The Clothes they Wore
19th and 20th Centuries

by Helen Herbert

illustrated by the author

Cambridge University Press

Cambridge
New York New Rochelle
Melbourne Sydney

LIFE STYLES AND FASHION Until quite recently, fashion had always been led by Kings and Queens, aristocrats and other rich and important people. They meant their clothes to show that they were above the common people. But from the end of the First World War, in 1918, style began to be influenced by the fashion designers of Paris, Milan, New York and London, and, as the 1930's started, by film personalities, and later by pop stars.

Sometimes it is easy to see why dresses were worn, say, longer or shorter; shortage of material, for instance, forced hemlines up during the Second World War, 1939–45; from the 1950's the new, freer styles made corsets less and less necessary. But for other fashions, like high or low waistlines, there often seems to be little reason except whim.

With advanced mass-production methods from the 1930's onwards ordinary people could buy copies of designer fashions from chain stores within weeks of the big fashion shows.

In the late 1970's, people became more selective and more aware of what suited them – helped by dozens of books and magazines advising them on creating their own style. They no longer relied slavishly on designers to create their total look, as they had up to the 1960's. 'Street fashion' – styles developed by teenagers themselves in towns and cities – had also had its effect on designer clothes.

In the 1980's royalty has again had some influence on fashion, with many women copying the lace and ruffles worn by Princess Diana. People are trying to keep their youthful shapes by exercise, including sport, jogging and aerobics. As the leisure time has increased, and because of repeated warnings by doctors about the dangers of being overweight, it has become fashionable to be physically active.

This book shows some of the changes in fashion and lifestyles in the last 180 years and some of the events which brought them about.

THE EARLY 19TH CENTURY – ROMANTIC STYLES

Fashions in Britain before the 19th century had usually followed those of France. But Britain was at war with France and had been since 1777, and it was partly due to this that a particular British style of dress developed. This was romantic, as was the mood of the time, partly influenced by the poetry of the popular young writers Byron and Shelley. The style of women's clothes was simple. They wore soft, delicate gowns of fine cotton with high waists, inspired by Ancient Greek and Roman dress. Women wearing these gowns were said to look as though they had just stepped out of bed. The style actually made them look helpless and childish. Trimmings became increasingly rich. Some dresses had frills and puffed sleeves; people wore feathered bonnets and expensive Kashmir shawls from India. Copies of these shawls were soon being made at Paisley in Scotland, and before long were actually called 'paisley' shawls. They must have been welcome, as such flimsy dresses were not at all warm, especially as they were sometimes dampened to make them cling. Underwear was not particularly warm either, and, to avoid the embarrassment of men knowing about women's underwear, this was always made by female dressmakers.

While women dressed in a more and more feminine way, men's clothes remained definitely masculine. During the years of the Napoleonic wars, from 1803 to 1815, men's clothes were much influenced by military uniforms. A long coat with lots of buttons, and pantaloons tucked into leather boots with a peak just below the knee at the front, was the fashion for the stylish man. He had short hair and side-whiskers, and wore a top hat.

'Beau' Brummell, a well-known dandy of the time, started a fashion for wearing a cut-away plain-coloured coat with tightly fitting breeches tucked into riding boots. He prided himself that not a wrinkle could be seen on his clothes. Primary colours were everyone's favourites, and a typical outfit might be a blue coat and yellow breeches with a crimson waistcoat. With this sort of 'peacock plumage' Brummell wore elaborate neckcloths which must have taken ages to arrange over his frilled shirt. He spent so much on clothes that in 1819 he had to flee to France to escape his creditors, most of whom were tailors, shirtmakers, hatters and bootmakers.

THE HOURGLASS SHAPE AND BEYOND

As women squeezed their bodies into the fashionable hourglass shape of the mid-1820's, corsets became a must. To make her waist look tiny, the fashion-conscious woman would make her wide skirts stand out with lots of petticoats and a bustle. Her huge sleeves had down-filled pillows in them, and because of their shape were called leg-of-mutton sleeves. Little girls were dressed like their mothers, except that their dresses were shorter, revealing white linen trousers, which were worn instead of petticoats. Even small girls had to wear corsets – not much fun to play games in! Changes in travel affected the sort of clothes people wore. From 1815 John McAdam, a Scottish engineer, started to build roads made of crushed stone which were soon known as 'macadam' roads. Travel by coach now became far more comfortable than before and so the middle-classes travelled more. Because it was very cold riding on top of a coach – there is a tale of a coachman actually freezing to death while driving through a blizzard – a practical greatcoat with layers of capes was designed and soon became fashionable.

New, shorter and very full skirts became popular in the mid-1830's. They were supported by layers of petticoats, and the feet were revealed. The ideal was a pair of tiny feet, shod in the smallest and narrowest flat satin shoes that the wearer could squeeze into! To balance all this width, women wore their hair in elaborate styles, sometimes using many metres of ribbon, and combs and feathers as well.

Men wore frock coats with huge rolled, padded collars folded back to reveal frilly shirts and patterned waistcoats. Skin-tight trousers – known as 'unmentionables' – were flared at the foot over the wearer's boots. Men looked very dashing, with bushy side-whiskers and curled hair topped by tall shiny hats.

SOBERING UP

In the later 1830's the extreme styles of previous years changed. The enormous leg-of-mutton sleeves were replaced by tighter sleeves, but frocks still kept the long, sloping shoulderline which went so well with the flatteringly fitted bodice. Skirts had lots of tiny pleats at the waist and began to be longer, covering the ankles. Bonnets, shaped like old-fashioned coal-scuttles, were pulled in closely to the chin making it impossible to see a woman's face except from the front! Since small flowered patterns were again fashionable, dresses from the previous century could be taken to pieces and remade in up-to-date styles. Even poorer women could sometimes afford the new cheap cotton dresses printed with tiny flower or geometric patterns.

Coal-scuttle bonnet

Fashion continued its trend towards more sober clothes for men, and more modest and subdued dress for women. A growing influence in English social life were the new middle classes, who did not wish to appear showy and overdressed. Men had to look respectable and gentlemanly, and their wives tried to show the social importance of their menfolk by looking both modestly fragile and incapable of doing anything. The only exceptions were genteel occupations such as the everlasting embroidery, which 'saved' them from the sin of idleness! As the middle class woman wore tight corsets and a great number of starched petticoats, it is not surprising that she did not lead a tremendously active life, as she must have been exhausted by almost any activity.

Queen Victoria came to the throne in 1837. Albert, her Prince Consort, was a serious-minded man and had a sobering effect on fashion. He was one of the first to wear the black frock-coat which, in America, was named the Albert Coat.

Small boy in a dress

Boy in a Sailor Suit

QUEEN VICTORIA'S INFLUENCE
When Queen Victoria came to the throne everything was done to make women look as short as possible – perhaps because she was very small. So shoes were flat, a bit like the ballet slippers we know now. Dresses at this time were made to stand out by numerous petticoats and a small horsehair bustle. Paisley shawls were again popular, sometimes so large as to make women look like dumpy sacks. Queen Victoria's love of Scotland led to the building of her palace at Balmoral, and made all things Scottish into fashion favourites. Tartan was worn not only by women – men's trousers and children's dresses were made of it too. Children sometimes wore complete kilted outfits known as 'Scotch Dress'.

Changes in fashion sometimes happen for strange reasons. In 1849 Marie Manning was tried for the murder of her husband. The case was widely reported in the newspapers and lasted a long time. She wore black satin throughout the trial and was eventually found guilty. Shiny black satin was out of fashion for years afterwards!

Emotional strain or even slight physical exertion often caused women to faint due to their tight corsets and heavy skirts. At the same time as women were restricted in this way the world around them was steaming ahead rapidly – railways were being built all over the countryside in Britain and Europe. Industry was expanding fast, and, unlike the middle class, working class girls worked for long hours in factories and shops.

Up to the age of 9 it was hard to tell small boys and small girls apart, as they all wore dresses, though the boys did have shorter hair and slightly less frivolous hats. At this period girls were wearing hats with crowns, while their mothers were still in bonnets, called 'poke bonnets', but these were not now pulled so close to the face. By 1850 people had become so set in their style of dress that it seemed fashion would never change.

HUGE HOOPED SKIRTS The Great Exhibition of 1851 at the Crystal Palace in London not only showed off British technology of the time but gave encouragement to international trade by including the products of other European countries, such as Germany and France, Britain's trade rivals. Commerce and trade were booming and women dressed more elaborately to show off their husbands' newly acquired wealth.

More and more petticoats were added under women's skirts. It must have been a relief when the hoop petticoat, or artificial crinoline, was invented. Tiers of steel hoops hung on tapes from the waist, and this allowed for free movement of the wearer's legs and for even wider skirts actually to feel comfortable.

These hooped skirts had one great disadvantage – in high winds they were hard to control. To avoid showing their legs – this was still considered rude – women took to wearing pantaloons edged with lace, sometimes reaching down to their ankles.

By 1850 dresses had become so ridiculously large that it was impossible for two women to fit on a sofa together! The male attitude to these exaggerated hoop skirts is shown in the 'Song of the Hoop' from *Harper's New Monthly Magazine* of 1857:

> "Sailing down the crowded street,
> Scraping everyone they meet,
> With a rushing whirlwind sound,
> Muffled belles around abound,
> Hoop! Hoop! Hoop!
> What a vast expansive swoop.'

When Mrs Amelia Bloomer arrived in Britain from America in 1851, she tried to convert women from their extravagant, impracticable hoops to her new costume . . . This was a simple bodice with an ample, below-the-knee skirt and baggy trousers underneath reaching to the ankles and edged in lace. But she did not get a favourable response, in fact she was ridiculed. Men thought that women were going to 'wear the trousers' – men were being threatened! Cartoonists had a wonderful time showing small, frightened men being bullied by enormous wives wearing bloomers.

Mrs Amelia Bloomer

RESTRICTION OR FREEDOM?

The new fashion magazines and paper patterns made fashion accessible to a wider public. Since the invention of the sewing machine, more dressmakers were earning a living making clothes for the middle classes and more women were making clothes at home.

By the middle of the 1860's, the crinoline became a 'half crinoline' – with lots of material gathered into a train at the back. By the 1870's fashion had dictated that the crinoline should be removed completely, perhaps because of its inconvenience. All the loops of material needed to be supported, so a bustle made of horsehair was worn. The 'Langtry' bustle, named after Lily Langtry, a famous actress, was advertised as being 'light, cool, easy to wear'. It was an extraordinary contraption – it had an arrangement of springs so that it could be raised when the lady sat down, and would spring back when she stood up!

A group of people who objected to the unhealthy and restrictive fashion of tight corsets and unnecessary layers of clothing banded together in the 1880's to form the Rational Dress Movement. These women began to wear loose dresses with full sleeves, and softer hairstyles. The Rational Dress Movement had a wide effect, as more women began to lead active lives.

WAR AFFECTS FASHION

At the beginning of the 20th century no-one could have guessed the enormous effect on fashion that the First World War was to have. The outbreak of war in 1914 stopped all extravagance in fashion. Women took part in the war effort, working in factories and driving buses and ambulances, and for this they needed more practical clothes. As fabric became scarce, so skirts were made tighter and rose to six inches above the floor, freeing the legs and ankles. Dull, dark colours and severe military styles were adopted for the duration. By the end of the war, in 1918, dresses were barrel-shaped, which later, in the 1920's, became the popular tube shape.

Men, who were tired of wearing uniform, rejected the military styles then in fashion, keeping only the famous trenchcoat. This was really a caped raincoat and was made by Burberry's of London, who still make coats like it today. These coats were so useful and practical that women started to wear them too.

During the war

After the war

THE ROARING TWENTIES 'The Roaring Twenties', as it is sometimes called, was a rather hysterical time of post-war enjoyment. 'Bright Young Things' – the wealthy, younger set – held wild parties and danced endlessly to the newly popular jazz bands. But for many people it was not a fun time. After a short boom in industry following the war, came the Depression, 'the slump', and with it growing unemployment. With the collapse of the American stock market in 1929, the fashion world suffered huge losses in sales and many companies were ruined.

For the middle and upper classes, however, fashion was still to be followed. Suddenly style dictated a boyish shape – helped by a 'flattener', a corset designed to flatten curves. The waist disappeared and clothes were draped from the shoulders. In 1925, scandalously, skirts rose to the knee! As was to be expected, this was denounced from the pulpit. A law was even passed in one state of America forbidding short skirts. But it all had no effect.

Young women started to cut their hair very short in a style called the Eton crop and wore close fitting 'cloche' hats low on their foreheads. Now they looked even more like boys.

    Men's fashion was slowly changing. Oxford undergraduates wore enormously wide, baggy trousers called 'Oxford bags'. This exaggerated trend did not last long, but men's trousers continued to be cut rather loose and wide and had waist pleats. As usual, these styles gradually filtered through to working class men, and this was helped by the appearance of chains of tailor's shops catering for the needs of men with modest incomes.

    Noel Coward, actor and playwright, had his own way of dressing. He was often photographed in a dressing gown of patterned silk, smoking a cigarette in a long, ebony holder. These mannerisms were met with a good deal of suspicion, because many people thought it unmanly for men to wear anything so unusual. People at this time were flocking in their thousands to the new cinemas and it was not long before Hollywood film stars, like Greta Garbo, were having a lot of influence on the fashion-conscious woman.

THE MASS MARKET THIRTIES AND WARTIME SHORTAGES

By the 1930's styles were less extravagant, and late in the decade the ideal shape was wider, with padded shoulders, narrower waists and skirts just below the knee.

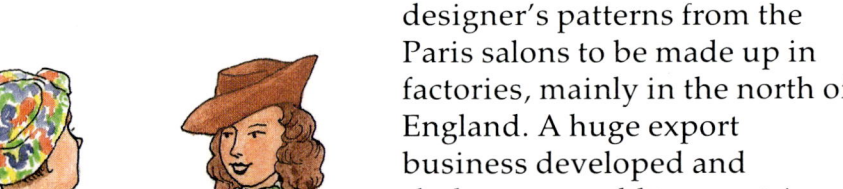

The Depression of the 1930's brought the fashions of the rich and of the street closer together. Ever since 1875, when *Myra's Journal* had published Paris couture patterns, women had been able to run up fashionable clothes on the new sewing machines. Now manufacturers rushed to buy designer's patterns from the Paris salons to be made up in factories, mainly in the north of England. A huge export business developed and clothes were sold to countries all over the world.

In September 1939, what everyone had dreaded happened – the Second World War broke out. Almost immediately rationing was introduced. You could only buy what your standard allocation of 'coupons' would allow, unless you bought things on the illegal 'Black Market'. This applied as much to clothes and fabrics as to food. The 'Utility' scheme, introduced by the Government soon afterwards, made maximum use of all available materials in the manufacture of household goods and clothes. It strictly regulated the length and width of skirts and controlled every other aspect of manufacture. In spite of this, there was choice in styles, with more attention paid to details. Dresses were made up to look like suits, because less material was needed. Many women worked in factories and had to wear their shoulder-length hair in headscarves for safety. To brighten their dull outfits, these 'turbans' were often of coloured, patterned fabrics. Silk stockings, almost impossible to get, were replaced by socks or by leg make-up, which tended to streak in the rain, with a mock 'seam' drawn down the back of the calf with an eyebrow pencil. No-one went anywhere without their gas mask in its canister or box-like case.

By the end of the war, in 1945, wartime shortages had made British and American people rely mainly on their own designers, and the Paris fashion houses could never again have the power and prestige they had enjoyed before.

Women, particularly, breathed a sigh of relief as rationing ended in the late 1940's and a new wardrobe of clothes became possible. Factories had become efficient in the mass production of uniforms, so Britain could easily produce the large quantities of new civilian outfits which would now be needed.

The military influence on the beret

One way of re-using a man's top hat

Crochet hat – 'could be made in a day'

THE 'NEW LOOK', TO THE TEEN SCENE

Women now wanted more feminine styles, so they took up the pre-war fashion of full skirts and womanly curves. Christian Dior, a famous French designer, caused a sensation with his 'New Look' exhibited in Paris in 1947. It had a softly rounded shoulder line, a tight waist and a very full, calf-length skirt held out with petticoats. The well dressed woman of the 1950's wore gloves and hats, some of

which were huge and shaped almost like flying saucers. Men reverted to Edwardian style clothes, and sports jackets and dark blazers with flannel trousers became more popular than dark, formal suits.

Living standards improved for everyone in the 1950's. More trade meant that industry created more jobs, so more people had money to spend on fashion clothes. In Britain and America, teenage girls were beginning to want their own fashion and not a copy of their mothers'. Some young fashions came from America – wide skirts with net petticoats, flat shoes, jeans and sloppy jerseys. The 'beatnik' look came from British street fashion and was influenced by pop stars. Most young working class men, having no trouble finding work, had plenty of money to spend. Some adapted the Edwardian style and wore long, loose jackets and tight drainpipe trousers with thick, crêpe-soled shoes. Elvis Presley, the Rock and Roll star, sang 'Don't tread on my blue suede shoes!' Men dressed in these fashions were known as 'Teddy Boys'.

These fashions were revolutionary – for the first time in history working class people were developing their own fashions, and not simply following the upper class lead.

One of the longest lasting fashions had begun to appear in the streets – jeans. These tough, hardwearing trousers, made out of blue denim, seemed almost indestructible. It was a stroke of American genius which made these garments fashionable with all classes of people. A few years previously they had been worn only by unskilled workmen and a few cowboys!

Teddy boy and girl jiving

Beatnik wearing jeans

THE SWINGING SIXTIES

In 1957 Harold Macmillan, the British Prime Minister, said in a speech to the nation 'You've never had it so good', and it was true that there was more widespread prosperity than ever before. Certainly the 'Swinging Sixties' saw big social changes for everyone.

For the first time in history, fashion was geared to the young and manufacturers had difficulty in producing enough for the growing needs of teenagers. Teenage boys queued outside shops that sold copies of the new ankle boots, called Chelsea boots, worn by the Beatles pop group. In the early sixties Mary Quant designed cheap, waistless, sleeveless dresses, with matching coats, boots, stockings, handbags and even make-up, creating a total look which was lively and young and very different to anything which had gone before.

By 1965 skirts had become mini-length, making the all-in-one tights more practical wear than stockings and suspender belts, which would have shown. Stocking factories began to make millions of pairs of tights in hundreds of colours and designs – patterned, appliquéd and textured. Trouser suits were worn by women for the office – and, for the first time, in businesslike pinstripes. Artificial materials, such as transparent plastics, were now widely used because they were cheap. There were even paper dresses and throwaway paper pants. The emphasis was on cheap clothes so that a new outfit could be bought almost every week at little cost.

Men's styles were also far more daring, with coloured shirts – pink was thought most outrageous! Suits had exaggerated, wide lapels and flared trousers. Brightly coloured T-shirts were worn by both sexes. Carnaby Street in London's Soho became a shopping place for the young, full of colour and loud music.

The ideology, and the clothes, of the gentle Hippies, or Flower People, arrived on the scene from America. Young men with long hair and unkempt beards and women with flowers in their waist-length hair often wore long, flowing kaftans. Jeans had to be faded and frayed, and many Hippies went barefoot.

THE GENTLE AND THE ROUGH   As the 1970's began, many people longed for a simpler way of life. Healthier diets and back-to-nature living became popular. Natural materials were increasingly used – Laura Ashley started making cotton country print dresses which would have been popular in the 1820's! This swing towards natural fibres and away from man-made ones was costly and not everyone could afford a real wool jersey instead of an acrylic or nylon one.

   Men's clothes became more casual, even for office work. The sports jacket was a favourite, and so was the army-influenced bomber jacket in leather or suede. Unisex clothes started to appear, with some women dressed for work in masculine-cut suits. This coincided with women increasingly competing with men for the same jobs.

At the end of the seventies 'Punk Rockers' shocked many people by their aggressive, anti-fashion styles. 'Bondage' trousers with chains linking the legs, safety pins in the ears – and even through the nose – with clothes deliberately cut and torn, were seen on the streets. But these street fashions were soon modified by designers and, ironically, became high fashion. The Punk hairstyles, spiky and dyed in rainbow colours, lingered through the seventies and the eighties. The 'Mohican' – where the sides of the head were shaved to a huge crest of hair on top which was then dyed in vivid colours – was an extreme style.

In the 1980's people wanted more comfortable and practical clothes. The craze for jogging and keep-fit, which started in the seventies, made the stretchy track suit fashionable and popular for everyday wear. Workmen's boiler suits and dungarees, too, were adapted to be worn by everyone, and were made up in all sorts of different materials and colours.

What will happen to fashion next? Lack of jobs and shortage of money might lead to us all becoming more inventive in our fashion ideas. Perhaps we will all be wearing the warm, strong, but very light synthetic materials developed for space travel? Or will there be a reaction against technology and a return to hand-woven cloth?

PLACES TO VISIT

The Museum of Costume
Assembly Rooms
Bath

Cheltenham Art Gallery and Museum
Clarence Street
Cheltenham

Museum of Childhood
38 High Street
Edinburgh

Royal Scottish Museum
Chambers Street
Edinburgh

Art Gallery and Museum
Kelvingrove
Glasgow

Bethnal Green Museum of Childhood
Cambridge Heath Road
London

Victoria and Albert Museum
South Kensington
London

The Museum of London
London Wall
London

The Gallery of English Costume
Platt Hall
Rusholme
Manchester

Costume Galleries
Castle Howard
York

York Castle Museum
Tower Street
York